indian

bar-be-cue

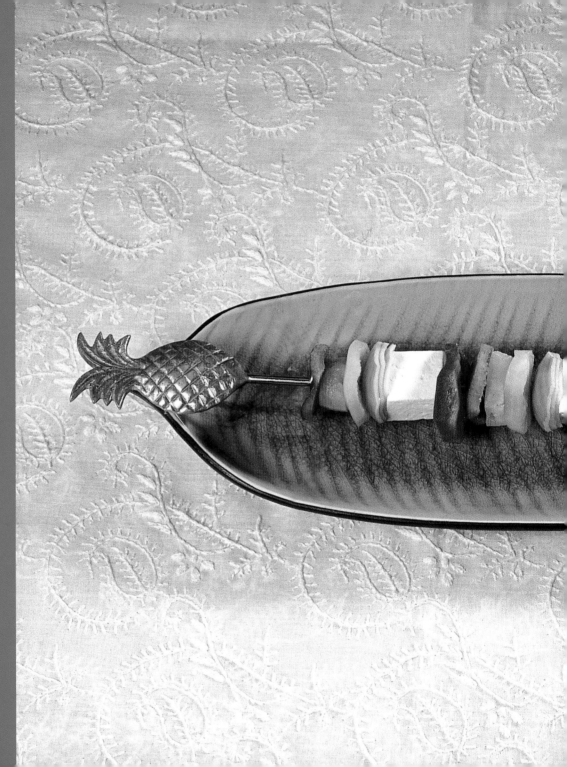

ISBN: 978-81-7436-498-2

© Roli & Janssen BV 2007
Published in India by
Roli Books in arrangement
with Roli & Janssen BV
M-75, G. K.-II Market
New Delhi 110 048, India.
Ph: ++91-11-29212271
Fax: ++91-11-29217185
Email: roli@vsnl.com
Website: rolibooks.com

Printed and bound at
Singapore

indian
bar-be-cue

Lustre Press
Roli Books

contents

7 *Introduction*

8 *Barbecue Equipment*

10 *Basic Techniques*

11 *Cooking Methods*

13 Vegetarian

27 Fish & Other Seafood

43 Chicken

67 Lamb

91 Accompaniments

96 *Index*

introduction

Tandoori is India's best known export, a cuisine that suits the international palate comfortably, since it is largely meat-based, lightly spiced, and easy to both cook and serve. So named because the food is cooked in a tandoor (large coal-fired oven), it is easily adaptable to the oven, the electrical grill or the microwave. Tandoori is akin to the western barbecue, but with more delicate flavours and with marinades which enhance the flavour of the principle ingredient. The process of cooking is fast and efficient, and it is only the preparation that may take a while. Tandoori or barbecued food may be served as starters, or may form a part of the main course, eaten with roti, and mint and coriander chutney.

Indian cuisine has a range and variety that is almost extraordinary, with each region contributing its own flavour. Modern Indian cooking borrows selectively from these diverse styles, assimilates and adapts them to suit the palate. The richness of Indian food, therefore continues to grow.

Barbecuing is no longer simply skewered meat kebabs. Besides making healthy side dishes, there is no limit to the range of delicious vegetable and fruit dishes that can form main courses such as potatoes, capsicum, tomatoes cooked on skewers or wrapped in foil parcels. A delight to all barbecue enthusiasts.

barbecue equipment

There is a vast range of accessories and barbecue equipment that one has to keep in mind while barbecuing. Some are very sensible and should be considered essentials:

— The charcoal barbecues: are the most common type as it is extremely mobile.

— The gas barbecues: are more eco-friendly as they create no smoke. However, a gas barbecue is not as mobile as the charcoal one as it has to be connected to a gas cylinder.

— Barbecue gloves: one must keep well-insulated gloves when cooking on a barbecue. When buying these gloves, check that they are long enough to protect the wrist.

— Barbecue apron: the person cooking should always wear an apron made from strong fabric to protect the clothing and bare skin from splashes of hot fat. The apron must not contain any artificial fibers since these are highly flammable.

— Bellows: these are used to deliver the oxygen needed when lighting charcoal. Alternatively, a folded newspaper can be used to do the job.

— Poker: when cooking with charcoal, you need a charcoal to distribute the charcoal and glowing embers. The handle should be well insulated so that it does not become too hot from heat conducted by the metal.

— Barbecue tongs: these are very important as they make it easy to turn pieces of meat of any size.

- Roasting rack: is useful for chickens and larger roasts, as it is easier to manipulate.
- For carving meat: a carving fork, a large sharp kitchen knife, and a chopping board with a groove all around to catch the juices is a must have.
- Stong aluminium foil should always be available when barbecuing. For example, juicy vegetables like tomatoes cannot be cooked easily on a grid. They should be wrapped in aluminium foil and then cooked on the grid.
- Brushes for basting the food with oil or marinade is an essential equipment to have.
- Metal and wooden skewers for making kebabs.
- A wire brush for cleaning the grid and fire bowl.
- A bucket of water in case the fire gets out of control.

basic techniques

A few important tips must be kept in mind to ensure a perfect barbecue:

The grid

The grid should be placed about 2-3" above the fire and it should always be cleaned before use. A wire brush or crumpled up piece of foil can be used to remove the food residue left behind on the grid. Grease the grid with oil before cooking to prevent food from sticking.

Temperature

The temperature of electric or gas barbecues can be easily controlled by turning the knob. Charcoal is a little trickier. If charcoal is too hot, cook the food near the edge of the grid. If the temperature is too low, put the food to one side, knock the ash off the charcoal and increase the rate of combustion with a few puffs of the bellows.

Cooking in aluminium foil

If you want the food to brown on the outside, wrap it only very loosely in foil. To prevent the food from browning at all, wrap it tightly in foil.

Cooking in charcoal embers

Food wrapped in foil can also be placed directly on the charcoal. Potatoes are particularly suitable for cooking in this way.

Cooking on a skewer

Food cooked on a skewer can be cooked very evenly since they are easy to turn. Brush the meat frequently with fat or marinade during the cooking process.

cooking methods

Some methods involved in cooking barbecued food are as follows:

Grilling
Cooking the food directly over the heat.

Sautéing
Food can be cooked on a barbecue in a heavy-based skillet in the same way as on an ordinary stove. The pan must be oiled well and the fire should be very hot. Do not use a pan with a wooden or plastic handle, as it might be damaged by the heat.

Roasting
Large pieces of meat can be roasted by moving the charcoal to one side and enclosing the grid with a cover or lid so that the heat comes from all sides. It is easier to cook food on a skewer since they are easy to turn. It is important that the food should be arranged evenly and stuck firmly on the skewer. Brush the meat frequently with fat or marinade during the cooking process.

vegetarian

Barbecued potato rolls

Baida kebab

Preparation time: 40 min. Cooking time: 10-15 min. Serves: 4

Ingredients:

Eggs	11
Potatoes, boiled, mashed	200 gm / 7 oz
Garam masala	1 tsp / 3 gm
Chaat masala	1 tsp / 3 gm
Breadcrumbs	$^1/_2$ cup / 60 gm / 2 oz
Salt	$1^1/_2$ tsp / 6 gm
Red chilli powder	1 tsp / 3 gm
Ginger (*adrak*), chopped	1 tbsp / $7^1/_2$ gm
Green chillies, chopped	1 tsp
Green coriander (*hara dhaniya*), chopped	1 tbsp / 4 gm
Butter for basting	2 tbsp / 30 gm / 1 oz

Method:

1. Boil 10 eggs, grate and keep aside.
2. Mix together the grated eggs, mashed potatoes, garam masala, *chaat* masala, breadcrumbs, salt, red chilli powder, ginger, green chillies, green coriander, and the raw egg.
3. Divide this mixture into 5 equal portions
4. Wrap each portion along the length of skewers with wet hands leaving a 1" gap between each. Barbecue for 5-10 minutes or roast in the oven.
5. Remove and baste with butter. Roast further for 3-5 minutes or until cooked.
6. Remove from skewers and serve hot with mint and coriander chutney (see p. 95).

vegetarian

Skewered cottage cheese kebabs

Paneer seekh kebab

Preparation time: 15 min. Cooking time: 15 min. Serves: 4-5

Ingredients:

Cottage cheese (*paneer*), grated	1 kg / 2.2 lb
Green chillies, chopped	30 gm / 1 oz
Onions, grated	2
Ginger (*adrak*), coarsely ground	1 tbsp / 7^1/$_2$ gm
Green coriander (*hara dhaniya*), chopped	2 tbsp / 8 gm
Black pepper (*kali mirch*) powder	2 tsp / 3 gm
Cumin (*jeera*) powder	1 tsp / 3 gm
Red chilli powder	1 tsp / 3 gm
Salt to taste	
Cornflour	2 tbsp / 20 gm
Butter for basting	

Method:

1. Mix all the ingredients, adding the cornflour in the end and knead well.

2. With wet hands wrap the cottage cheese mixture around the skewers to form a 4-5"-long kebab and 2" apart.

3. Roast in a preheated (150°C / 300°F) oven / tandoor / charcoal grill for 5-6 minutes, basting occasionally with melted butter.

4. Serve hot with salad and mint and coriander chutney (see p.95).

vegetarian

Stuffed capsicum

Bharwan Shimla mirch

Preparation time: 30 min. Cooking time: 10 min. Serves: 4-5

Ingredients:

Capsicum (*Shimla mirch*), large	6
Butter / Vegetable oil	1 tbsp / 15 ml
Spring onions, chopped	120 gm / 4 oz
Green coriander (*hara dhaniya*), chopped	1 tbsp / 4 gm
Cottage cheese (*paneer*), grated	250 gm / 9 oz
Salt to taste	
Chaat masala	1 tbsp / 9 gm
Green chillies, chopped	4
Cumin (*jeera*) powder	2 tsp / 6 gm

Method:

1. Slice each capsicum from the top. Scoop out the seeds and keep capsicum cup and top aside.
2. Heat the butter / oil in a pan; stir-fry the spring onions. Add the remaining ingredients and cook for 4-5 minutes. Remove from heat.
3. Fill the cottage cheese mixture into the capsicum cups and cover the top with the capsicum slice. Secure with toothpicks.
4. Preheat oven to 150°C / 300°F. Place stuffed capsicums on a baking tray or skewer carefully and grill on charcoal for 8-10 minutes till the skin develops golden brown spots. Remove toothpicks and serve hot.

vegetarian

Cottage cheese cubes flavoured with fenugreek

Kastoori paneer tikka

Preparation time: 2¼ hrs. Cooking time: 10 min. Serves: 4-5

Ingredients:

Cottage cheese (*paneer*), cut into 1½'' cubes	1 kg / 2.2 lb
Black cumin (*shah jeera*) seeds	1 tsp / 2½ gm
White pepper (*safed mirch*) powder	1 tsp / 3 gm
Garam masala	2 tsp / 6 gm
Lemon (*nimbu*) juice	5 tsp / 25 ml
Salt to taste	
Cottage cheese, grated	50 gm / 1¾ oz
Cream	½ cup / 120 ml / 4 fl oz
Yoghurt (*dahi*), hung	¾ cup / 180 gm / 6 oz
Gram flour (*besan*) / Cornflour	2 tbsp / 20 gm
Dry fenugreek (*kasoori methi*)	4 tsp / 2 gm
Chaat masala (optional)	2 tsp / 6 gm
Ginger-garlic (*adrak-lasan*) paste	2 tbsp / 36 gm
Red chilli powder	2 tsp / 6 gm
Butter for basting	

Method:

1. Mix black cumin seeds, white pepper powder, garam masala, 4 tsp lemon juice, salt, and grated cottage cheese together. Refrigerate for 1 hour.
2. Whisk the remaining ingredients (except butter) to a fine batter. Add the cottage cheese cubes, mix well and marinate for at least 1 hour.
3. Preheat the oven to 150°C / 300°F. Thread the cubes 1'' apart on a skewer. Roast in an oven / tandoor / charcoal grill for 5-6 minutes. Baste with butter.
4. Serve hot sprinkled with *chaat* masala and remaining lemon juice, accompanied with mint and coriander chutney (see p. 95).

Cottage cheese slices layered with mint and coriander chutney

Dum saunfia tikka

Preparation time: 2¹/₂ hrs. Cooking time: 10 min. Serves: 4

Ingredients:

Cottage cheese (*paneer*)	900 gm / 2 lb
Yoghurt (*dahi*)	¹/₂ cup / 120 gm / 4 oz
Cream	¹/₄ cup / 60 ml / 2 fl oz
Red chilli powder	1 tsp / 3 gm
Yellow chilli powder	1 tbsp / 9 gm
White pepper (*safed mirch*) powder	1 tsp / 3 gm
Carom (*ajwain*) seeds	1 tsp / 2¹/₂ gm
Salt to taste	
Raisins (*kishmish*)	3 tbsp / 30 gm / 1 oz
Fennel (*moti saunf*), powdered	2 tsp / 6 gm
Sugar	1 tbsp / 14 gm
Mint and coriander chutney (see p. 95)	¹/₂ cup / 100 gm / 3¹/₂ oz

Method:

1. Hang the yoghurt in a muslin cloth for 2 hours, till whey is drained. Add cream, red chilli powder, yellow chilli powder, white pepper powder, carom seeds, and salt; mix well.

2. Add raisins, fennel powder, and sugar to the mint and coriander chutney.

3. Cut cottage cheese into 1¹/₂'' slices. Slit the cubes and spread the chutney mixture.

4. Press halves together again.

5. Marinade the cheese cubes in the yoghurt-cream-spice mixture for 15 minutes.

6. Skewer the pieces and cook in a preheated oven at 140°C / 275°F for 5 minutes. Serve hot as a snack.

vegetarian

Stuffed potato rectangles

Tandoori aloo

Preparation time: 20 min. Cooking time: 15 min. Serves: 4

Ingredients:

Potatoes, large, peeled	8 / 1 kg / 2.2 lb
Vegetable oil for frying	
Salt to taste	
Red chilli powder	1 tsp / 3 gm
Garam masala	a pinch
Lemon (*nimbu*) juice	1 tsp / 5 ml
Cashew nuts (*kaju*), broken	5-10
Raisins (*kishmish*)	1 tbsp / 10 gm
Ghee	2 tsp / 10 gm
Cheese, grated	20 gm
Green coriander (*hara dhaniya*), chopped	1 tbsp / 4 gm
Chaat masala	¹/₂ tsp

Method:

1. Scoop out the centre of the potatoes leaving thin walls at the sides.
2. Fry the potato shells and the scoops separately. Do not let them change colour but let the sides become crisp.
3. Cool the scooped out portion of the potatoes and mash. Add salt, red chilli powder, garam masala, lemon juice, cashew nuts, raisins, and ghee.
4. Stuff the mixture into the potato cases.
5. Arrange 4 pieces on one skewer and sprinkle grated cheese on top. Grill till golden brown in colour.
6. Sprinkle with green coriander and *chaat* masala, serve hot.

vegetarian

Roasted batter fried cauliflower

Tandoori phool

Preparation time: 45 min. Cooking time: 20 min. Serves: 4

Ingredients:

Cauliflowers *(phool gobi)*, broken into florets, washed, dried	2 / 800 gm / 28 oz
Salt to taste	
Chaat masala	4 tsp / 12 gm
Juice of lemons *(nimbu)*	2
Gram flour *(besan)*	4 tbsp / 40 gm
Red chilli powder	2 tsp / 6 gm
Vegetable oil for frying and basting	
Cucumber *(khira)*, sliced	1
Tomatoes, cut into wedges	2

Method:

1. Marinate the florets in a mixture of salt, *chaat* masala, and lemon juice for 30 minutes.
2. Mix gram flour with $1/2$ cup water into a smooth batter. Season with salt and red chilli powder.
3. Heat the oil in a frying pan; dip the florets in the batter and lower gently into the hot oil; fry on low heat. Remove. Once the florets are cool, cut into pieces.
4. Skewer the pieces and roast in a tandoor for 5-6 minutes till golden brown or roast in a preheated oven at 140°C / 275°F for 10 minutes. Baste with oil while roasting. Remove from skewers and serve with cucumber and tomato wedges.

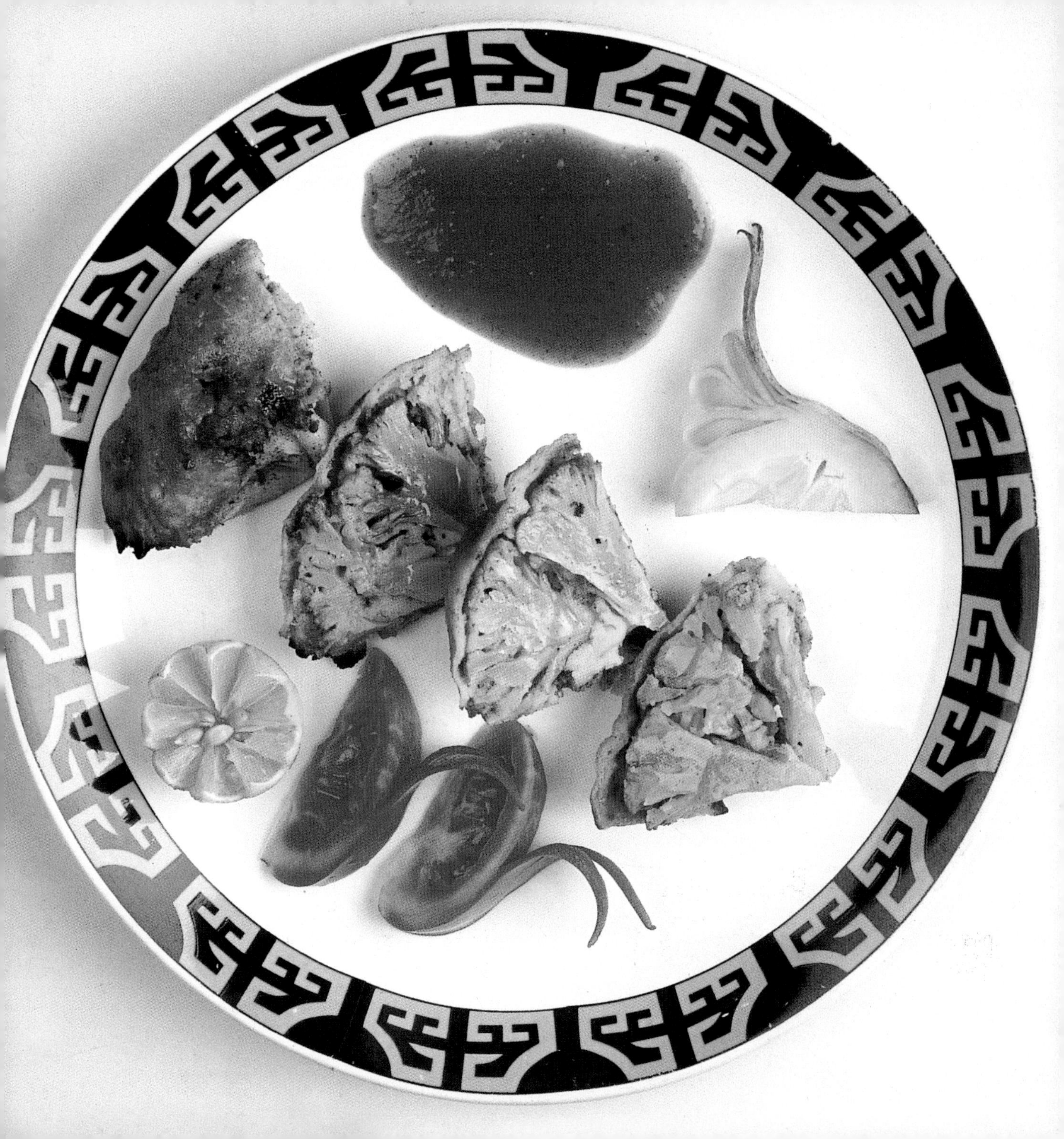

fish & other
seafood

Fish tikkas

Mahi tikka

Preparation time: 2½ hrs. Cooking time: 15-20 min. Serves: 4

Ingredients:

Fish, cut into boneless pieces	1 kg / 2.2 lb
Ghee	½ cup / 100 gm / 3½ oz
Onions, sliced	½ cup / 50 gm / 1¾ oz
Garlic (*lasan*), chopped	3 tbsp / 18 gm
Salt to taste	
Red chilli powder	2 tbsp / 18 gm
Coriander (*dhaniya*) powder	2 tsp / 6 gm
Cumin (*jeera*) powder	1 tsp / 3 gm
Turmeric (*haldi*) powder	1 tsp / 3 gm
Yoghurt (*dahi*)	½ cup / 120 gm / 4 oz
Butter for basting	

Method:

1. Heat the ghee in a pan; fry the onions till brown. Remove, drain excess ghee and blend the onions to a smooth paste.
2. In the same pan, fry the garlic and keep aside.
3. Allow the ghee to cool. Mix the onion paste, garlic, the remaining ingredients (except butter), and fish pieces with the ghee and keep aside for 2 hours.
4. Skewer the fish pieces and roast in a tandoor / oven / grill for 5-10 minutes. Remove, baste with butter and cook further for 3-5 minutes.
5. Remove from skewers and serve hot.

Smoked fish chunks

Saloni machchi tikka

Preparation time: 40 min. Cooking time: 15-20 min. Serves: 4

Ingredients:

Fish, cut into boneless pieces, washed, pat-dry	800 gm / 28 oz
For the marinade:	
Salt	1 tbsp
White pepper (*safed mirch*) powder	1 tsp / 3 gm
Fenugreek (*methi*) powder	1/2 tsp
Turmeric (*haldi*) powder	1/2 tsp / 1 1/2 gm
Red chilli powder	1 1/2 tsp / 4 1/2 gm
Garam masala	1 tsp / 3 gm
Clove (*laung*) powder	a pinch
Ginger-garlic (*adrak-lasan*) paste	5 tsp / 30 gm / 1 oz
Yoghurt (*dahi*), drained	2 tsp / 10 gm
Vinegar (*sirka*)	3/4 cup / 150 ml / 5 fl oz
Cream	1/2 cup / 120 gm / 4 fl oz
Mustard oil	4 tbsp / 60 ml / 2 fl oz
Cloves (*laung*)	16
Charcoal piece, live	1
Vegetable oil for basting	

Method:

1. **For the marinade,** mix all the ingredients together and rub into the fish pieces; keep aside.

2. Make a well in the centre and put mustard oil and cloves. Place the live charcoal piece in the oil and cover the bowl with a lid. Seal the lid so that the smoke does not escape. Keep aside for 30 minutes.

3. Remove the lid, skewer the fish and roast in a medium hot tandoor for 5-6 minutes. Remove from the tandoor and allow excess marinade to drip off.

4. Baste with oil and roast again for 2 minutes until done.

5. Serve hot with mint and coriander chutney (see p. 95).

Barbecued prawns in a rich and creamy marinade

Jhinga Mehrunisa

Preparation time: 40 min. Cooking time: 10 min. Serves: 4

Ingredients:

Prawns, shelled, deveined	1.5 kg / 3.3 lb
Vinegar (*sirka*)	3 tbsp / 45 ml / 1¹/₂ fl oz
Salt to taste	
For the marinade:	
Lemon (*nimbu*) juice	4 tsp / 20 ml
Yoghurt (*dahi*)	1 cup / 250 gm / 9 oz
Cream	1 cup / 250 ml / 9 fl oz
White pepper (*safed mirch*) powder	1¹/₂ tsp / 4¹/₂ gm
Cheese, grated	80 gm / 2³/₄ oz
Dry fenugreek (*kasoori methi*) powder	2 tsp / 1 gm
Ginger-garlic (*adrak-lasan*) paste	2 tbsp / 36 gm / 1¹/₄ oz
Garam masala	1 tsp / 4¹/₄ gm
Saffron (*kesar*)	a few strands
Butter for basting	

Method:

1. Wash the prawns with vinegar and salt water. Drain and pat dry.
2. **For the marinade,** mix all the ingredients together. Rub into the prawns and marinate for 30 minutes.
3. Skewer the prawns and roast in a moderately hot tandoor for 6-8 minutes. Remove from tandoor and allow excess marinade to drip off.
4. Baste lightly with butter and roast again for 2-3 minutes. Remove from skewers and serve with mint and coriander chutney (see p. 95).

fish & other seafood

Saffron flavoured fish rolls stuffed with prawns

Jalpari kebab

Preparation time: 40 min. Cooking time: 20 min. Serves: 4

Ingredients:

Fish fillets, thin	12
Prawns, shelled, deveined	225 gm / 8 oz
Ginger-garlic (*adrak-lasan*) paste	5 tsp / 30 gm / 1 oz
Mango pickle masala	5 tsp / 25 gm
Carom (*ajwain*) seeds	1 tsp / 2$^{1}/_{2}$ gm
White pepper (*safed mirch*) powder	1 tsp / 3 gm
Garam masala	2 tsp / 6 gm
Salt to taste	
Red chilli powder	1 tsp / 3 gm
Lemon (*nimbu*) juice	1 tsp / 5 ml
Vegetable oil	4 tsp / 20 ml
Yoghurt (*dahi*), drained	$^{3}/_{4}$ cup / 180 gm / 6 oz
Cream	2 tbsp / 40 ml / 1$^{1}/_{2}$ fl oz
Saffron (*kesar*)	a few strands
Green cardamom (*choti elaichi*) powder	a pinch
Water	4 cups / 1 lt / 32 fl oz

Method:

1. Extract juice from ginger-garlic paste and keep aside.
2. Clean the fish fillets and prawns. Pat dry with a cloth.
3. Make a marinade with ginger-garlic juice, mango pickle masala, half of carom seeds, white pepper powder, garam masala, salt, red chilli powder, lemon juice, and oil.
4. Marinate the fish fillets in the prepared marinade and keep aside for 5 minutes.
5. Prepare second marinade of yoghurt, cream, saffron, green cardamom powder, and remaining half of other ingredients. Keep aside.

Handy Hint:

Fish with firm flesh and jumbo prawns are ideally suited for grilling on a barbecue. You can tell if fish is fresh by its shiny colour (fish that are less fresh have a rather lack-luster appearance). The eyes must be clear and the scales should not detach too easily.

6. Put one fish fillet flat on a tabletop. Place a prawn at one end of the fillet and roll the fillet. Wrap it tightly with cling wrap or aluminium foil.

7. Boil water in a pot and cook the rolls for 10 minutes keeping the pot covered.

8. Drain the water and place the rolls under running water for a minute. Remove the foil.

9. Marinate the rolls in the second marinade for 5 minutes.

10. Skewer the rolls and roast in hot tandoor or in an oven (150-180°C / 300-350°F) for 10 minutes.

11. Remove from skewers, transfer to a serving platter and serve hot with mint and coriander chutney (see p. 95).

Tandoori fish in yoghurt marinade

Dahi machchi

Preparation time: 3½ hrs. Cooking time: 20 min. Serves: 4-5

Ingredients:

River or sea fish	
(with single centre bone)	5 (400 gm / 14 oz each)
Salt to taste	
Malt vinegar (*sirka*)	3 tbsp / 45 ml / 1½ fl oz
Yoghurt (*dahi*), drained	1 cup / 250 gm / 9 oz
Black pepper (*kali mirch*) powder	2 tsp / 6 gm
Fennel (*moti saunf*)	2 tsp / 5 gm
Garlic (*lasan*) paste	5 tsp / 30 gm / 1 oz
Ghee	3 tbsp / 45 gm / 1½ oz
Ginger (*adrak*) paste	5 tsp / 30 gm / 1 oz
Gram flour (*besan*)	4 tbsp / 40 gm / 1½ oz
Lemon (*nimbu*) juice	5 tsp / 25 ml
Red chilli powder	4 tsp / 12 gm
Turmeric (*haldi*) powder	2 tsp / 6 gm
Butter for basting	2½ tbsp / 50 gm / 1¾ oz

Method:

1. Marinate fish in vinegar and salt.
2. In a bowl, mix yoghurt with the remaining ingredients (except butter) and make a fine paste.
3. Marinate the fish in this paste and leave to stand for 2-3 hours.
4. Preheat the oven to 180°C / 350°F.
5. Skewer the fish from mouth to tail, 1½" apart. Roast in the oven for 12-15 minutes.
6. Baste with butter. Remove and hang the skewers to let excess marinade drip off.
7. Serve hot, garnished with slices of cucumber, tomato and onion rings; accompanied by mint and coriander chutney (see p. 95).

Tandoori prawns

Tandoori jhinga

Preparation time: 2 hrs. Cooking time: 15 min. Serves: 4

Ingredients:

Prawns, king size	12
Ginger (*adrak*) paste	1$\frac{1}{2}$ tsp / 9 gm
Garlic (*lasan*) paste	2 tsp / 12 gm
Lemon (*nimbu*) juice	2 tbsp / 30 ml / 1 fl oz
Yoghurt (*dahi*)	1 cup / 250 gm / 9 oz
Gram flour (*besan*)	2 tbsp / 20 gm
Salt to taste	
Carom (*ajwain*) seeds	1 tsp / 2$\frac{1}{2}$ gm
Red chilli powder	1 tsp / 3 gm
Garam masala	1 tsp / 3 gm
Turmeric (*haldi*) powder	$\frac{1}{2}$ tsp / 1$\frac{1}{2}$ gm
Vegetable oil for basting	
Chaat masala to taste	

Method:

1. Mix ginger-garlic pastes and 1 tbsp lemon juice together; rub into the prawns and keep aside.
2. Whisk together yoghurt, gram flour, salt, carom seeds, red chilli powder, garam masala, and turmeric powder into a smooth paste. Marinate the prawns in the paste for at least 2 hours.
3. Skewer the prawns and cook in a preheated (150°C / 300°F) oven / tandoor / grill / for about 12-15 minutes or till almost done.
4. Hang skewers for 3-5 minutes to allow excess marinade to drip off. Baste with oil and roast again for 3-5 minutes or till golden brown.
5. Sprinkle *chaat* masala and remaining lemon juice. Serve hot with a salad of your choice.

fish & other seafood

38

Roasted prawns coated with sesame seeds

Jhinga nisha

Preparation time: 1 ¹/₂ hrs. Cooking time: 20 min. Serves: 4

Ingredients:

Prawns	8
Lemon (*nimbu*) juice	1 tsp / 5 ml
Ginger-garlic (*adrak-lasan*) paste	4 tsp / 24 gm
Salt to taste	
Sesame (*til*) seeds	3 tsp / 9 gm
Yoghurt (*dahi*)	4 tsp / 20 gm
Cheddar cheese	3 tsp / 15 gm
Cinnamon (*dalchini*) powder	1 tsp / 3 gm
Dry fenugreek (*kasoori methi*) leaves	1 tsp
White pepper (*safed mirch*) powder	1 tsp / 3 gm
Green chillies	6
Clove (*laung*) powder	1 tsp / 3 gm
Chaat masala	1 tsp / 3 gm

Method:

1. Rub lemon juice, ginger-garlic paste, and salt on the prawns and keep aside for half an hour.
2. Roast the sesame seeds and crush to a powder.
3. Beat the yoghurt in a bowl and add the remaining ingredients (except *chaat* masala).
4. Rub this mixture on the prawns and keep in a cool place for an hour. Preheat the oven to 150°C / 300°F.
5. Skewer the prawns and roast till light golden in colour. Apply the sesame seed powder over the prawns and roast again for 2 minutes. Sprinkle with *chaat* masala and lemon juice.

Tandoori lobsters

Preparation time: 4¹/₂ hrs. Cooking time: 10 min. Serves: 4-5

Ingredients:

Lobsters, medium-sized, halved	4
Ginger (*adrak*) paste	4 tsp / 24 gm
Garlic (*lasan*) paste	4 tsp / 24 gm
Carom (*ajwain*) seeds	¹/₂ tsp
Malt vinegar (*sirka*)	¹/₂ cup / 100 ml / 3¹/₂ fl oz
Salt to taste	
Yoghurt (*dahi*), drained	1 cup / 250 gm / 9 oz
White pepper (*safed mirch*) powder	1 tsp / 3 gm
Garam masala	2 tsp / 6 gm
Egg	1
Cottage cheese (*paneer*)	60 gm / 2 oz
Gram flour (*besan*)	3 tbsp / 30 gm / 1 oz
Mustard oil	4 tbsp / 60 ml / 2 fl oz
Red chilli paste	1 tsp / 5 gm

Method:

1. Shell and devein the lobsters. Wash, dry the shells and dip in hot oil. Drain and keep aside.
2. Marinate lobsters in ginger and garlic pastes, carom seeds, vinegar, and salt for an hour.
3. Whisk yoghurt in a large bowl. Add the remaining ingredients; coat the lobsters with this mixture; keep aside for 3 hours.
4. Skewer the lobsters 1'' apart. Keep a tray underneath to collect the excess drippings. Roast in a medium-hot tandoor / oven for 5 minutes. Baste with butter and roast again for 2 minutes.
5. Place the lobster in the shell; garnish with lettuce, tomato slices, and onion rings. Serve hot.

chicken

Delicate chicken kebabs with a hint of fenugreek

Murgh bannu kebab

Preparation time: 45 min. Cooking time: 20 min. Serves: 4

Ingredients:

Chicken, cut into boneless cubes, washed, dried	900 gm / 2 lb
Salt	2 tsp / 6 gm
Dry fenugreek (*kasoori methi*) powder	1 tsp
Ginger-garlic (*adrak-lasan*) paste	2 tbsp / 36 gm / 1¼ oz
Green chillies, chopped	2 tsp
Green coriander (*hara dhaniya*), chopped	1 tbsp / 4 gm
Vinegar (*sirka*)	1 tsp / 5 ml
Vegetable oil	5 tbsp / 75 ml / 2½ oz
Gram flour (*besan*), sieved	5 tsp / 15 gm
Breadcrumbs, fresh	2½ tbsp / 15 gm
Egg yolks, whisked	6

Method:

1. Mix salt, dry fenugreek powder, ginger-garlic paste, green chillies, green coriander, and vinegar together; rub into the chicken. Refrigerate for 15 minutes.

2. Heat the oil in a pan; stir-fry the gram flour till a pleasing smell emanates. Add chicken cubes and sauté on low heat for 3-5 minutes till half cooked.

3. Add breadcrumbs and mix well. Remove and spread on a clean tabletop to cool.

4. Skewer the cubes 2" apart and roast in a tandoor till done. Bring the cubes close together and coat with egg yolk. Roast till the egg coating turns golden brown. Remove, garnish with onion rings and serve hot.

chicken

Cheesy chicken kebabs

Murgh Afghani kebab

Preparation time: 4¹/₂ hrs. Cooking time: 15 min. Serves: 4-5

Ingredients:

Chicken broiler, without skin, cut into 12 pieces	2 (750 gm / 26 oz each)
Salt to taste	
White pepper (*safed mirch*) powder	a pinch
Mace (*javitri*) powder	2¹/₂ tsp / 7¹/₂ gm
Ginger (*adrak*) paste	2 tbsp / 36 gm / 1¹/₄ oz
Garlic (*lasan*) paste	2 tbsp / 36 gm / 1¹/₄ oz
Malt vinegar (*sirka*)	¹/₄ cup / 50 ml / 1³/₄ oz
Yoghurt (*dahi*)	2 cups / 500 gm / 1.1 lb
Cheese, grated	100 gm / 3¹/₂ oz
Cream	3 tbsp / 60 ml / 2 fl oz
Green chillies, chopped	6
Green cardamom (*choti elaichi*)	1 tsp
Butter for basting	

Method:

1. Mix salt, white pepper, ¹/₂ tsp mace powder, ginger and garlic pastes with malt vinegar. Rub the mixture into chicken and marinate for an hour.

2. Mix the remaining ingredients (except butter). Transfer the marinated chicken into this yoghurt mixture. Keep aside for 3 hours.

3. Preheat the oven to 180°C / 350°F. Skewer the chicken, 1'' apart. Keep a tray underneath to collect the drippings. Roast in an oven / tandoor / grill for 10-12 minutes. Remove and hang the skewers to allow the excess marinade to drip off.

4. Baste with butter and roast for 3 more minutes. Serve hot with lemon wedges and *naan* or roti.

chicken

Chicken tikka marinated in cottage cheese

Murgh paneer tikka

Preparation time: 4 hrs. Cooking time: 15 min. Serves: 4-6

Ingredients:

Chicken breasts, cut into boneless cubes	1 kg / 2.2 lb
Lemon (*nimbu*) juice	1 tbsp / 15 ml
Garlic (*lasan*) paste	3 tbsp / 54 gm / 1³/₄ oz
Salt to taste	
Cottage cheese (*paneer*), grated	150 gm / 5 oz
Cream	4 tbsp / 80 ml / 2³/₄ oz
Cornflour	1¹/₂ tbsp / 15 gm
Green chilli paste	2 tsp / 10 gm
White pepper (*safed mirch*) powder	1 tsp / 3 gm
Green coriander (*hara dhaniya*), chopped	1 tbsp / 4 gm
Butter for basting	

Method:

1. Marinate chicken in lemon juice, garlic paste, and salt mixture for an hour.
2. Mix cottage cheese, cream, cornflour, green chilli paste, white pepper powder, and green coriander in a bowl; whisk till smooth. Marinate chicken in this mixture for at least 3 hours.
3. Skewer chicken 1'' apart and roast in a preheated (180°C / 350°F) oven / tandoor / grill for 8-10 minutes. Baste with butter and roast for another 3 minutes or until golden in colour.
4. Garnish with tomato, onion, and cucumber slices and serve hot with mint and coriander chutney (see p. 95).

chicken

Creamy chicken tikkas

Murgh malai tikka

Preparation time: 4 hrs. Cooking time: 12 min. Serves: 4-6

Ingredients:

Chicken breasts, cut into boneless cubes	1 kg / 2.2 lb
Garlic (*lasan*) paste	2 tbsp / 36 gm / 1¼ oz
Ginger (*adrak*) paste	2 tbsp / 36 gm / 1¼ oz
Salt to taste	
White pepper (*safed mirch*) powder	1 tsp / 3 gm
Egg, whisked	1
Cheddar cheese, grated	60 gm / 2 oz
Green chillies, deseeded, finely chopped	8
Green coriander (*hara dhaniya*), finely chopped	1 cup / 50 gm / 1¾ oz
Mace-nutmeg (*javitri-jaiphal*) powder	½ tsp
Cornflour	1 tbsp / 10 gm
Cream	¾ cup / 180 ml / 6 fl oz
Vegetable oil / Butter for basting	

Method:

1. Rub garlic-ginger pastes, salt, and white pepper into the chicken cubes. Keep aside for 15 minutes.
2. Mix the remaining ingredients together (except oil / butter); coat the chicken with this prepared mixture. Marinate for at least 3 hours.
3. Skewer the chicken cubes 1'' apart and roast in a preheated (140°C / 275°F) oven / grill / tandoor for 5-8 minutes. Hang the skewers for 3-5 minutes to allow excess marinade to drip off; brush with oil and roast again for 3 minutes.
4. Garnish with green coriander, and lemon wedges and serve hot with mint and coriander chutney (see p. 95).

Chicken drumsticks with beetroot

Chukandri tangri kebab

Preparation time: 3 hrs. Cooking time: 20 min. Serves: 4-5

Ingredients:

Chicken drumsticks, without skin	15
For the first marinade:	
Beetroot (*chukandar*), finely grated	150 gm / 5 gm
Lemon (*nimbu*) juice	2 tbsp / 30 ml / 1 fl oz
Salt to taste	
For the second marinade:	
Yoghurt (*dahi*), whisked	³/₄ cup / 180 gm / 6 oz
Black cumin (*shah jeera*) seeds	2 tsp / 5 gm
Cream	4 tbsp / 80 ml / 2³/₄ fl oz
Garam masala	2 tsp / 6 gm
Ginger (*adrak*) paste	2 tbsp / 36 gm / 1¹/₄ oz
Garlic (*lasan*) paste	2 tbsp / 36 gm / 1¹/₄ oz
Butter for basting	4 tsp / 20 gm

Method:

1. Make 2 deep incisions on each drumstick.
2. Mix all ingredients of first marinade and rub evenly over chicken legs. Marinate for 1 hour.
3. Mix all ingredients of second marinade. Marinate chicken in this mixture; refrigerate for 2-3 hours.
4. Preheat oven to 180°C / 350°C. Skewer the drumsticks 1'' apart. Keep a tray underneath to collect the drippings.
5. Roast in hot tandoor / oven / grill for about 10-15 minutes. Baste continuously with butter. Garnish with lemon wedges and parsley and serve hot on a bed of shredded cabbage.

chicken

Chicken drumsticks coated with cashew batter

Tangri kebab

Preparation time: 1 hr. Cooking time: 15-20 min. Serves: 4

Ingredients:

Chicken, drumsticks, cleaned	12
Ginger-garlic (*adrak-lasan*) paste	4 tsp / 24 gm
White pepper (*safed mirch*) powder	a pinch
Salt	1 tsp / 3 gm
Vinegar (*sirka*)	1 tsp / 5 ml
Yoghurt (*dahi*)	1 cup / 250 gm / 9 oz
Cream	$^3/_4$ cup / 180 ml / 6 fl oz
Ginger-garlic paste	2 tbsp / 36 gm / $1^1/_4$ oz
White pepper powder	1 tsp / 3 gm
Garam masala	2 tsp / 6 gm
Salt	$^1/_4$ tsp / $1^1/_4$ gm
Saffron (*kesar*)	a few strands
Vegetable oil for basting	
Eggs, whisked	4
Cashew nuts (*kaju*), finely ground	5 tbsp / 75 gm / $2^1/_2$ oz

Method:

1. Make 4-5 deep vertical incisions on the drumsticks.
2. Mix ginger-garlic paste, white pepper powder, salt, and vinegar together. Coat the drumsticks with this paste and rub into the slits. Refrigerate for 15 minutes.
3. Make a second marinade with yoghurt, cream, ginger-garlic paste, white pepper powder, garam masala, salt, and saffron.
4. Marinate the chicken in the prepared marinade and refrigerate for another 15 minutes.

chicken

5. Skewer the drumsticks and roast in a tandoor for 3-5 minutes till half cooked. Remove and hang for 2-3 minutes to allow the excess marinade to drip off.
6. Baste with oil / butter and roast till completely cooked.
7. Mix the cashew nut paste and eggs together. Coat the drumsticks with this batter and roast again till the egg has coagulated. Remove from skewers.
8. Serve hot with mint and coriander chutney (see p. 95).

Barbecued chicken

Murgh Kandhari

Preparation time: 4-5 hrs. Cooking time: 15 min. Serves: 4-5

Ingredients:

Chicken broiler, without skin	2 (600 gm / 22 oz each)
Red chilli powder	2 tsp / 6 gm
Lemon (*nimbu*) juice	3 tbsp / 45 ml / 1^1/$_2$ fl oz
Pomegranate (*anar*) juice	3 tbsp / 45 ml / 1^1/$_2$ fl oz
Yoghurt (*dahi*), hung, whisked	1 cup / 250 gm / 9 oz
Ginger (*adrak*) paste	2 tbsp / 36 gm / 1^1/$_4$ oz
Garlic (*lasan*) paste	2 tbsp / 36 gm / 1^1/$_4$ oz
Black cumin (*shah jeera*) seeds	2 tsp / 5 gm
Black pepper (*kali mirch*) powder	1 tsp / 3 gm
Garam masala	2 tsp / 6 gm
Salt to taste	
Saffron (*kesar*)	1 gm
Double cream	4 tbsp / 80 ml / 2^3/$_4$ fl oz
Butter for basting	

Method:

1. Make 3 deep incisions each on sides of breast and thigh and 2 on each drumstick.
2. Mix red chilli powder, lemon juice, and pomegranate juice together; rub over the chicken evenly. Marinate for 2 hours and refrigerate.
3. Mix yoghurt with remaining ingredients (except butter). Marinate chicken in this mixture for 2-3 hours more. Refrigerate.
4. Preheat the oven / tandoor / grill to 180°C / 350°F. Skewer chicken from tail to head, leaving a gap of at last 1^1/$_2$''. Roast for 10 minutes. Remove, hang the skewers to let the excess moisture drip. Baste with butter and roast again for 4-5 minutes. Serve.

chicken

Cardamom flavoured chicken drumsticks

Neza kebab

Preparation time: 40 min. Cooking time: 25 min. Serves: 4

Ingredients:

Chicken, drumsticks	900 gm / 2 lb
For the marinade:	
Ginger-garlic (*adrak-lasan*) paste	5 tbsp / 90 gm / 3 oz
Salt	1^1/$_2$ tsp / 4^1/$_2$ gm
White pepper (*safed mirch*) powder	2 tsp / 6 gm
Garam masala	2 tsp / 6 gm
Dry fenugreek (*kasoori methi*) powder	1 tsp
Vinegar (*sirka*)	4 tsp / 20 ml
Green coriander (*hara dhaniya*), chopped	2 cups / 100 gm / 3^1/$_2$ oz
Green cardamom (*choti elaichi*) powder	2 tsp / 6 gm
Vegetable oil	4 tbsp / 60 ml / 2 fl oz
Gram flour (*besan*)	3 cups / 300 gm / 11 oz
Eggs, whisked	4
Cream	1 cup / 240 ml / 8 fl oz
Butter for basting	

Method:

1. Wash and clean the chicken drumsticks. Remove the thigh bone from the flesh. Do not remove it completely.

2. **For the marinade,** mix all the ingredients together and rub into the chicken. Marinate for 20 minutes.

3. Heat the oil in a pan; add gram flour and stir-fry on low heat till a pleasing smell emanates. Remove from heat and transfer to a mixing bowl to cool.

4. Add 1 egg and blend to make a smooth paste; add cream and mix well.

5. Add the remaining eggs to the mixture and mix thoroughly. Coat the chicken drumsticks with this marinade and keep aside for 20 minutes.

6. Skewer the drumsticks once along the bone and once through the thigh flesh. Cook in a tandoor for about 8-10 minutes or till slightly coloured. Remove and let excess marinade drip off.

7. Baste lightly with butter and roast again for 2-3 minutes or till completely done.

8. Remove from skewers onto a serving platter. Serve hot garnished with lemon wedges, cucumber and tomato pieces, and onion rings.

Skewered chicken

Tandoori murgh

Preparation time: 3¹/₂ hrs. Cooking time: 15-20 min. Serves: 4-5

Ingredients:

Chicken, whole, skinned	2 (600 gm / 22 oz each)
Salt to taste	
Red chilli powder	1 tsp / 3 gm
Lemon (*nimbu*) juice	3 tbsp / 45 ml / 1¹/₂ fl oz
Yoghurt (*dahi*)	¹/₂ cup / 120 gm / 4 oz
Cream	¹/₂ cup / 120 ml / 4 fl oz
Ginger-garlic (*adrak-lasan*) paste	2 tbsp / 36 gm / 1¹/₄ oz
Cumin (*jeera*) powder	1 tsp / 3 gm
Garam masala	1 tsp / 3 gm
Saffron (*kesar*)	a pinch
Orange colour	a drop
Vegetable oil / Butter for basting	
Chaat masala	1 tsp / 3 gm

Method:

1. Clean the chicken and make deep incisions on the breasts, thighs, and drumsticks.
2. Mix salt, red chilli powder, and lemon juice together. Rub this paste into the chicken evenly. Keep aside for half an hour.
3. Whisk yoghurt, cream, and remaining ingredients (except the last two) to make a smooth paste. Coat the chicken with this mixture. Marinate for 2¹/₂-3 hours.
4. Skewer the chicken leaving a gap of 3-4''. Roast in a moderately hot tandoor / grill / oven for 8-10 minutes. Remove, baste with butter / oil and roast for another 3-4 minutes. Cut into pieces, sprinkle *chaat* masala and serve hot.

chicken

Chicken breasts stuffed with minced lamb

Murgh chakori

Preparation time: 40 min. Cooking time: 30 min. Serves: 4

Ingredients:

Chicken, breasts	8
Lamb, minced	250 gm / 9 oz
Black cumin (*shah jeera*) seeds	1 tsp / 2^1/$_2$ gm
Dry ginger (*sonth*) powder	1 tsp / 3 gm
Fennel (*moti saunf*) powder	2 tsp / 6 gm
Cumin (*jeera*) powder	1 tsp / 3 gm
Red chilli powder	1 tsp / 3 gm
Coriander (*dhaniya*) powder	1 tsp / 3 gm
Salt	2 tsp / 6 gm
Yoghurt (*dahi*)	^{1}/$_4$ cup / 60 gm / 2 oz
Asafoetida (*hing*)	a pinch
Vegetable oil	1 cup / 250 ml / 8 fl oz
Water	1 cup / 250 ml / 8 fl oz
For the marinade:	
Yoghurt (*dahi*), drained	2 cups / 500 gm / 1.1 lb
Salt to taste	
Cream	^{1}/$_2$ cup / 120 ml / 4 fl oz
Red chilli powder	1 tsp / 3 gm
Vinegar (*sirka*)	1^1/$_2$ tsp / 8 ml
Coriander powder	1 tsp / 3 gm

Method:

1. Clean the chicken breasts, slit open from one side and flatten. Keep aside.
2. Blend together the lamb mince, black cumin seeds, dry ginger powder, fennel powder, cumin powder, red chilli powder, coriander powder, salt, yoghurt, and asafoetida.
3. Divide the mince mixture equally into balls. In a pan, heat the oil and water in equal quantities, reduce heat and immerse the balls into the pan. Cover and cook for about 20 minutes.
4. Stuff the prepared meat balls into the chicken breasts. Wrap the chicken breasts firmly with silver foil. Poach for 15 minutes.
5. Remove from heat and unwrap the chicken breast from the foil and allow to cool.

6. **For the marinade**, blend yoghurt, salt, cream, red chilli powder, vinegar, and coriander powder. Keep aside.
7. Marinate the chicken breasts with the prepared marinade and keep aside for 15 minutes.
8. Skewer the chicken breasts and cook in a tandoor for 5-10 minutes or until golden yellow.
9. Remove from the skewers and serve hot, accompanied by tandoori roti.

chicken

61

Stuffed tandoori drumsticks

Bharwan tangri

Preparation time: 1 hr. Cooking time: 15 min. Serves: 4

Ingredients:

Chicken drumsticks	8
White pepper (*safed mirch*) powder	1 tsp / 3 gm
Salt to taste	
Ginger (*adrak*) paste	1 tsp / 6 gm
Garlic (*lasan*) paste	1 tsp / 6 gm
For the filling:	
Cottage cheese (*paneer*), mashed	150 gm / 5 oz
Green chillies, finely chopped	4
Green coriander (*hara dhaniya*), finely chopped	1 tbsp / 4 gm
Cumin (*jeera*) powder	1 tsp / 3 gm
Yellow chilli powder	$^1/_2$ tsp / $1^1/_2$ gm
Cashew nuts (*kaju*), finely chopped	1 tbsp / 15 gm
Salt to taste	
For the coating:	
Cream	2 tbsp / 40 ml / $1^1/_2$ fl oz
Cheese, grated	1 tbsp / 15 gm
Cornflour	1 tbsp / 10 gm
Butter for basting	

Method:

1. Clean the drumsticks. Make an incision along the lower half of the drumsticks, taking care not to cut through the other side. Carefully open the flap for the filling.

2. Mix white pepper, salt, ginger and garlic pastes; rub evenly over the drumsticks. Marinate for 30 minutes.

3. **For the filling,** mix cottage cheese, green chillies, green coriander, cumin powder, yellow chilli powder, cashew nuts, and salt together.

4. Put some filling into the flap of the marinated drumstick. Secure with a toothpick. Similarly, prepare the other drumsticks and refrigerate for 15 minutes.

chicken

Handy Hint:

There is a common mis-conception that food must be constantly prodded with various utensils in order to cook properly. If you constantly pierce your steaks and chicken legs, juices will escape and you'll end up with a tough piece of leather.

5. **For the coating,** whisk the cream, cheese, and cornflour into a smooth paste. Coat each drumstick evenly with this paste.
6. Preheat oven / tandoor / grill to 180°C / 350°F. Skewer the drumsticks and roast for 8-10 minutes, basting occasionally with butter.
7. Remove skewers and hang for 3-4 minutes to let the excess marinade drip off.
8. Roast again for 3-4 minutes till golden. Serve hot, with mint and coriander chutney (see p. 95) and salad.

Chicken kebabs flavoured with fenugreek

Kastoori kebab

Preparation time: 1 hr. Cooking time: 15 min. Serves: 4-5

Ingredients:

Chicken breasts, cleaned, skinned, deboned, cut each into 2 pieces	12
For the marinade: mix together	
Ginger (*adrak*) paste	3 tbsp / 54 gm / 1³/₄ oz
Garlic (*lasan*) paste	3 tbsp / 54 gm / 1³/₄ oz
Dry fenugreek (*kasoori methi*) leaves	2 tbsp / 3 gm
White pepper (*safed mirch*) powder	1 tsp / 3 gm
Salt to taste	
Lemon (*nimbu*) juice	3 tbsp / 45 ml / 1¹/₂ fl oz
Butter	4 tbsp / 80 gm / 2³/₄ oz
Vegetable oil	2 tsp / 10 ml
Gram flour (*besan*)	1 tbsp / 10 gm
Breadcrumbs	1¹/₂ tbsp / 22 gm
Ginger, chopped	2 tbsp / 15 gm
Green coriander (*hara dhaniya*), chopped	1 cup / 50 gm / 1³/₄ oz
Black cumin (*shah jeera*) seeds	1 tsp / 2¹/₂ gm
Saffron (*kesar*)	¹/₂ gm
Egg yolks	3
Green cardamom (*choti elaichi*) powder	1 tsp / 3 gm
Lemon (*nimbu*) juice to taste	

Method:

1. **For the marinade**, rub the mixture into the chicken. Marinate for 1 hour.

2. Heat the butter and oil; add gram flour and stir on medium heat until golden. Divide this into two portions.

3. To one portion add breadcrumbs, ginger, green coriander, and marinated chicken. Mix well.

4. Preheat oven to 150°C / 300°F. To the second portion add black cumin seeds, saffron, and egg yolks; whisk the batter thoroughly.

5. Skewer 6 pieces together. Leave a gap of 1¹/₂" and then skewer the next lot. Coat each with the gram flour batter. Roast for 8-10 minutes. Remove and sprinkle with green cardamom powder and lemon juice. Serve hot.

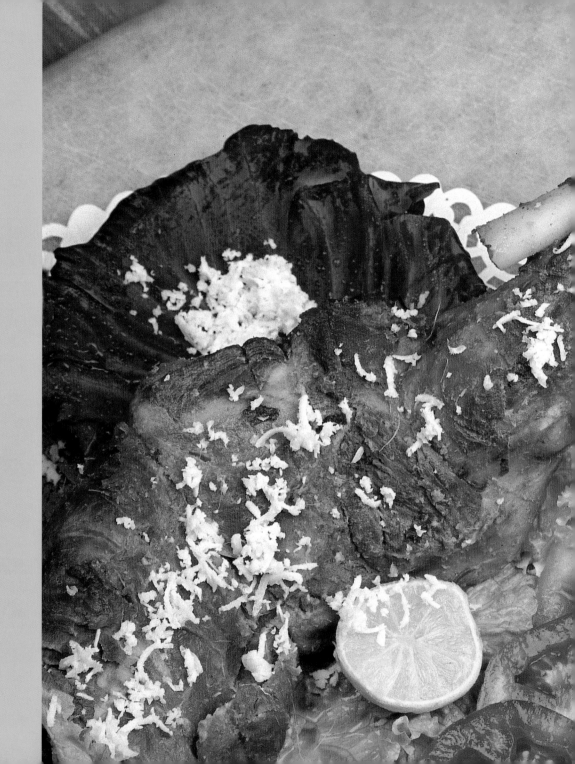

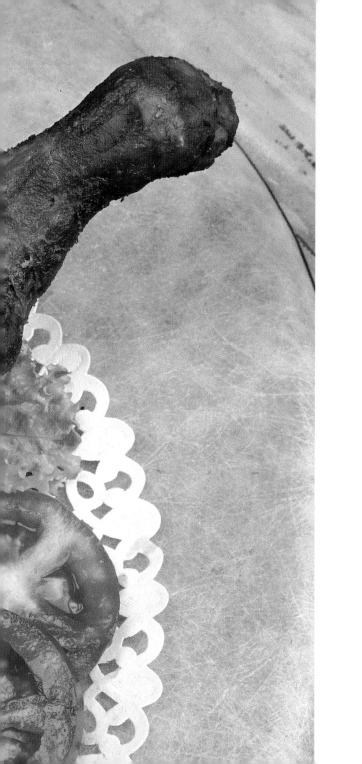

lamb

Spicy and aromatic lamb chunks

Shola kebab

Preparation time: 2 hrs. Cooking time: 15-20 min. Serves: 4

Ingredients:

Lamb, cut into boneless pieces	900 gm / 2 lb
Salt	4 tsp / 12 gm
Red chilli powder	4 tsp / 12 gm
White pepper (*safed mirch*) powder	a pinch
Fenugreek (*methi*) powder	a pinch
Green cardamom (*choti elaichi*) powder	a pinch
Garam masala	2 tsp / 6 gm
Onion (*kalonji*) seeds, crushed	2 tsp / 6 gm
Fennel (*moti saunf*), crushed	a pinch
Mustard seeds (*rai*), crushed	a pinch
Cumin (*jeera*) seeds, crushed	a pinch
Coriander (*dhaniya*) seeds, crushed	a pinch
Ginger-garlic (*adrak-lasan*) paste	2 tbsp / 36 gm / 1^1/$_4$ oz
Raw papaya, grated	60 gm / 2 oz
Mustard oil	^{1}/$_2$ cup / 100 ml / 3^1/$_2$ fl oz
Vinegar (*sirka*)	4 tsp / 20 ml
Yoghurt (*dahi*)	^{1}/$_2$ cup / 120 gm / 4 oz
Butter for basting	4 tsp / 20 gm

Method:

1. Prepare the marinade by mixing all the ingredients (except butter) together.
2. Rub the mixture into the lamb pieces and keep aside for 1^1/$_2$ hours.
3. Skewer the lamb pieces and roast in a medium hot tandoor for 10-12 minutes. Baste with butter and roast again for 5 minutes.
4. Remove from skewers and serve hot.

lamb

Lamb kebabs stuffed with cheese

Sakhat kebab

Preparation time: 40 min. Cooking time: 20-25 min. Serves: 4

Ingredients:

Lamb, minced	900 gm / 2 lb
Salt	1 tsp / 3 gm
White pepper (*safed mirch*) powder	a pinch
Red chilli powder	¹/₂ tsp / 1¹/₂ gm
Fenugreek (*methi*) powder	a pinch
Ginger-garlic (*adrak-lasan*) paste	2 tbsp / 36 gm / 1¹/₄ oz
Green chillies, chopped	1¹/₂ tsp
Green coriander (*hara dhaniya*), chopped	1 tbsp / 4 gm
For the filling:	
Processed cheese, grated	120 gm / 4 oz
Green chillies, chopped	4 tsp
For the batter:	
Cornflour	7 tbsp / 70 gm / 2¹/₄ oz
Refined flour (*maida*)	7 tbsp / 70 gm / 2¹/₄ oz
Egg, whisked	1
Vinegar (*sirka*)	1 tsp / 5 ml
Salt to taste	
White pepper powder	a pinch
Ginger-garlic paste	1¹/₂ tsp / 9 gm
Water	1 cup / 250 ml / 8 fl oz
Vegetable oil for frying	

Method:

1. Mix the lamb mince with the next 7 ingredients. Refrigerate for 15 minutes.
2. Mix the filling ingredients together. Divide into 16 equal portions.
3. **For the batter,** mix cornflour with flour, egg, vinegar, salt, white pepper powder, ginger-garlic paste, and water.
4. Make 4'- long kebabs with the mince mixture and skewer in 4 equal parts. Roast in a tandoor for 5 minutes and remove. Allow to cool, remove from skewers in 4 pieces each.
5. Slit each kebab lengthwise and stuff the cheese mixture.
6. Dip the stuffed kebabs in the prepared batter and deep-fry in hot oil until crisp and golden brown.
7. Serve hot with mint and coriander chutney (see p. 95).

lamb

Cinnamon flavoured ribs

Ghar ke chaamp

Preparation time: 30 min. Cooking time: 30 min. Serves: 6-8

Ingredients:

Lamb ribs, double	900 gm / 2 lb
Ghee / Vegetable oil	¹/₂ cup / 120 ml / 4 fl oz
Onions, minced	3 cups
Cinnamon (*dalchini*), 1'' sticks	2
Salt to taste	
Sugar	2 tsp
Red chilli power	1 tsp / 3 gm
Malt vinegar (*sirka*)	¹/₂ cup / 100 ml / 3¹/₂ fl oz
Garam masala	1 tsp / 3 gm

Method:

1. Heat the oil in a deep-bottomed pan; add the onions and cinnamon sticks. Sauté until the onions become translucent. Add the ribs, stir and add one cup of warm water, salt, sugar, red chilli powder, vinegar, and garam masala, and bring to the boil.

2. Reduce the heat to low and cover the pan. Cook until the ribs are tender and very little gravy remains.

Spicy lamb steaks

Tandoori masala gosht

Preparation time: 2 hrs. Cooking time: 7-10 min. Serves: 4

Ingredients:

Lamb steaks (2"x 2")	8
For the marinade:	
Onion, minced	1
Garlic (*lasan*), crushed	1 tbsp / 18 gm
Green chilli paste	1 tbsp / 15 gm
Poppy seeds (*khus khus*), ground	1 tbsp / 15 gm
Garam masala	1 tbsp / 9 gm
Salt to taste	

Method:

1. **For the marinade,** mix onion, garlic, green chilli paste, poppy seed paste, garam masala, and salt together. Rub into the lamb steaks. Marinate for 2 hours.
2. Roast in a charcoal grill / tandoor till cooked as desired.
3. Serve hot, garnished with onion rings and accompanied by pickled green chillies.

Barbecued lamb liver and kidney covered with chicken mince

Kallan kebab

Preparation time: 1 hr. Cooking time: 20-25 min. Serves: 4

Ingredients:

Lamb, minced	250 gm / 9 oz
Lamb kidney, finely chopped	125 gm / 4 oz
Lamb liver, finely chopped	125 gm / 4 oz
Salt	1/2 tsp / 1 1/2 gm
Red chilli powder	2 tsp / 6 gm
Garam masala	1 tsp / 3 gm
Fenugreek (*methi*) powder	a pinch
Ginger-garlic (*adrak-lasan*) paste	2 tsp / 12 gm
Green coriander (*hara dhaniya*), chopped	1 tbsp / 4 gm
Green chillies, chopped	1 tsp
Chicken, minced	500 gm / 1.1 lb
Salt	1/2 tsp / 1 1/2 gm
White pepper (*safed mirch*) powder	1/2 tsp / 1 1/2 gm
Garam masala	a pinch
Fenugreek powder	a pinch
Ginger-garlic paste	1/2 tsp / 3 gm
Green coriander, chopped	1 tbsp / 4 gm
Butter for basting	4 tsp / 20 gm

Method:

1. Mix the lamb mince, kidney, liver, salt, red chilli powder, garam masala, fenugreek powder, ginger-garlic paste, green coriander, and green chillies together. Keep aside.
2. Skewer the lamb mixture and roast in a charcoal grill for 8-10 minutes. Remove the skewer to allow excess moisture to drip off. Keep aside for 3-5 minutes.
3. Mix chicken with the remaining ingredients (except butter).
4. Apply a coat of the chicken mixture evenly over the lamb kebabs and roast for 5-6 minutes.
5. Baste with butter and remove the kebabs from skewers in 4 equal portions. Serve with green salad.

Succulent lamb chunks coated with papaya and yoghurt

Peshawari kebab

Preparation time: 1¼ hrs. Cooking time: 30 min. Serves: 4

Ingredients:

Lamb, boneless, cut into 1″ cubes.	1 kg / 2.2 lb
For the marinade:	
Yoghurt *(dahi)*	½ cup / 120 gm / 4 oz
Raw papaya paste	2 tsp / 10 gm
Salt to taste	
Red chilli powder	2 tsp / 4 gm
Garam masala	1 tsp / 3 gm
Black cumin *(shah jeera)* seeds	1 tsp / 2½ gm
Ginger *(adrak)* paste	1 tbsp / 18 gm
Garlic *(lasan)* paste	1 tsp / 6 gm
Ghee for basting	
Chaat masala	1 tsp / 3 gm
Juice of lemon *(nimbu)*	1

Method:

1. **For the marinade**, mix all the ingredients and rub well into the lamb. Leave aside for an hour.
2. Skewer the meat pieces and cook in a tandoor till half done.
3. Remove and leave to cool for 10 minutes.
4. Baste with ghee and cook for 8 more minutes.
5. Sprinkle with *chaat* masala and lemon juice. Serve hot with green salad.

Spicy minced meat skewered and roasted

Seekh kebab

Preparation time: 45 min. Cooking time: 15 min. Serves: 4

Ingredients:

Lamb, minced	500 gm / 1.1 lb
Black cardamom (*badi elaichi*)	2
Black peppercorns (*sabut kali mirch*)	2 tsp / 8 gm
Cinnamon (*dalchini*) powder	¹/₂ tsp
Cloves (*laung*)	2
Coconut (*nariyal*), grated	1 tbsp / 4 gm
Cream	2 tbsp / 40 ml
Cumin (*jeera*) seeds	1 tsp / 2 gm
Garlic (*lasan*) paste	3 tsp / 18 gm
Ginger (*adrak*) paste	3 tsp / 18 gm
Gram flour (*besan*), roasted	3 tbsp / 30 gm / 1 oz
Mace (*javitri*) powder	¹/₂ tsp / 1¹/₂ gm
Vegetable oil	1 tbsp / 15 ml
Onion paste, browned	2 tbsp / 50 gm / 1³/₄ oz
Poppy seeds (*khus khus*)	2 tsp / 6 gm
Raw papaya paste	1 tbsp / 15 gm
Red chilli powder	1 tsp / 3 gm
Yoghurt (*dahi*)	2 tbsp / 60 gm / 2 oz

Method:

1. Mix mince with all the other ingredients. Knead well for 10 minutes. Let it stand for 10 minutes.

2. Moisten hands with water and mould the mixture around skewers pressing and shaping to about 5¹/₂''-long kebabs. Roast in a moderately hot tandoor for 12 minutes till they are browned uniformly.

3. The kebabs can also be slid off the skewers and cooked on fine wire mesh of the grilling rack in a charcoal gas grill. Do not turn too often as they may split. Serve hot with mint and coriander chutney (see p. 95).

lamb

78

Skewered lamb chops

Barah kebab

Preparation time: 4¹/₂ hrs. Cooking time: I hr. Serves: 4

Ingredients:

Lamb, chops and leg pieces	900 gm / 2 lb
For the marinade:	
Salt to taste	
Red chilli powder	2 tsp / 6 gm
Garam masala	4 tsp / 12 gm
Malt vinegar (*sirka*)	³/₄ cup / 150 ml / 5 fl oz
Ginger (*adrak*) paste	3 tbsp / 54 gm / 1³/₄ oz
Garlic (*lasan*) paste	3 tbsp / 54 gm / 1³/₄ oz
Raw papaya paste	4 tsp / 20 gm
or *Kachri* (tenderizer)	4 tsp / 20 gm
Black cumin (*shah jeera*) seeds	3 tbsp / 23 gm
Yoghurt (*dahi*)	¹/₄ cup / 60 gm / 2 oz
Vegetable oil for basting	

Method:

1. **For the marinade,** mix all the ingredients together and rub into the lamb. Keep aside for 4 hours or overnight.
2. Skewer the pieces 1'' apart and roast on a slow fire in a tandoor or charcoal grill for 15 minutes or till half done.
3. Stand at room temperature for 20 minutes. Baste with oil.
4. Roast or grill on slow fire for another 20 minutes till velvety brown.
5. Serve with onion rings and lemon wedges.

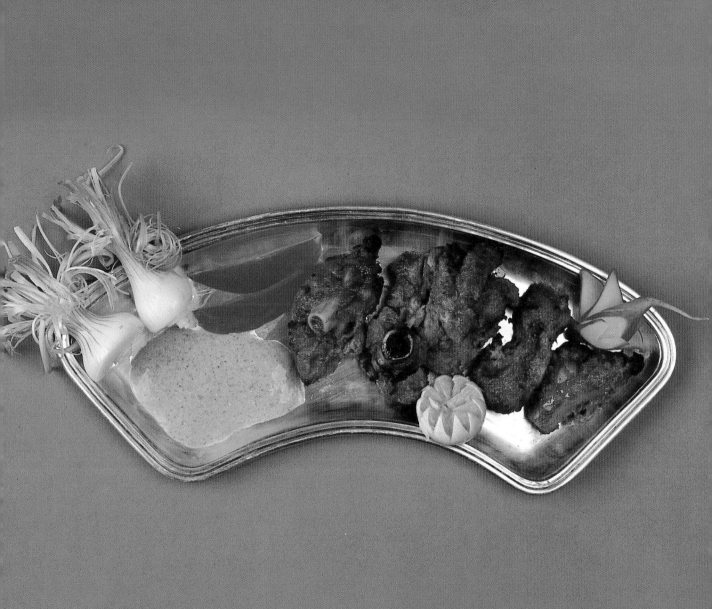

Thin meat slices roasted on skewers

Pasinda kebab

Preparation time: 3¹/₂ hrs. Cooking time: 15 min. Serves: 4

Ingredients:

Lean meat slab	450 gm / 1 lb
Blend together:	
Cloves (*laung*)	5
Green cardamom (*choti elaichi*)	5
Raw papaya paste	1¹/₂ tsp / 7¹/₂ gm
or *Kachri* (tenderizer)	1 tsp / 5 gm
Garlic (*lasan*) cloves, chopped	10
Onions, chopped	¹/₄ cup / 30 gm / 1 oz
Ginger (*adrak*), chopped	2" piece / 15 gm
Cumin (*jeera*) seeds	1 tsp / 2 gm
Coconut (*nariyal*), desiccated	2 tbsp / 8 gm
Nutmeg (*jaiphal*) powder	¹/₄ tsp
Black peppercorns (*sabut kali mirch*)	16
Poppy seeds (*khus khus*)	1 tsp / 3 gm
Yoghurt (*dahi*)	³/₄ cup / 180 gm / 6 oz
Red chilli powder	1 tsp / 3 gm
Salt to taste	
Butter for basting	

Method:

1. Cut meat into 3¹/₂" long, 1¹/₄" wide and ³/₄"-thick slices. Cut the slice into half without cutting through, leaving it intact at the end. Open the cut halves to make a single strip, approximately 6" long. Beat the joints with the back of a knife to flatten them a bit.

2. Blend all the ingredients together to a fine paste. Coat the strips with this mixture and marinate for 3 hours.

3. Weave the skewer in and out of the meat strips at 4 points, at regular intervals. Roast over an open charcoal fire or barbecue for 10 minutes. When one side is cooked, baste with butter and roast again for 3-5 minutes. Serve as a salad.

Melt-in-the-mouth skewered kebabs

Kakori kebabs

Preparation time: 30-40 min. Cooking time: 10 min. Serves: 4

Ingredients:

Lamb, finely minced (*keema*)	800 gm / 28 oz
Ginger-garlic (*adrak-lasan*) paste	1 tsp / 6 gm
Cashew nut (*kaju*) paste	3 tbsp / 45 gm / 1¹/₂ oz
Poppy seed (*khus khus*) paste	1 tbsp / 15 gm
Salt to taste	
Garam masala	1 tbsp / 9 gm
Yellow chilli powder	1 tbsp / 9 gm
Ghee	4 tsp / 20 gm
Melted butter for basting	

Method:

1. In a tray mix the lamb mince with all the ingredients except butter. Divide the mixture into 16 equal portions and shape each into a ball.
2. With moist hand spread each ball on the skewer. Grill over charcoal grill at a moderate temperature for 4-6 minutes. Baste with melted butter and further roast for 1-2 minutes.
3. Serve hot with choice of salad and chutney.

Tangy mint lamb chops

Khatta pudina chops

Preparation time: 4 hrs. Cooking time: 12-15 min. Serves: 4-5

Ingredients:

Lamb chops, cleaned	1 kg / 2.2 lb
Cumin (*jeera*) powder	1 tsp / 3 gm
White pepper (*safed mirch*)	1 tbsp / 9 gm
Garam masala	2 tsp / 6 gm
Lemon (*nimbu*) juice	5 tsp / 25 ml
Salt to taste	
Cream	4 tbsp / 80 ml
Yoghurt (*dahi*), drained	³/₄ cup / 180 gm / 6 oz
Mint and coriander chutney (see p. 95)	1¹/₄ cup / 250 gm / 9 oz
Cornflour	2 tbsp / 20 gm
Papaya paste (optional)	3 tbsp / 45 gm
Garlic (*lasan*) paste	1 tbsp / 18 gm
Ginger (*adrak*) paste	1 tbsp / 18 gm
Fenugreek (*methi*) powder	1 tsp / 3 gm
Vegetable oil for basting	

Method:

1. Mix cumin powder, white pepper, garam masala, lemon juice, and salt together. Rub the paste into the lamb chops and marinate for 1 hour.
2. Mix cream, yoghurt, mint and coriander chutney, and cornflour. Add the remaining ingredients (except oil) and whisk to a fine paste. Mix with lamb chops and marinate for another 2¹/₂-3 hours.
3. Skewer lamb chops 1'' apart and roast in a preheated (180°C / 350°F) oven / tandoor / charcoal grill for 8-10 minutes. Hang the skewers for a few minutes to allow excess marinade to drip off. Baste with oil and roast for another 4-5 minutes.
4. Sprinkle lemon juice, garnish with slices of cucumber, tomato, and onion; serve hot.

Ginger flavoured lamb chops

Adraki champen

Preparation time: 3-4 hrs. Cooking time: 10-15 min. Serves: 5

Ingredients:

Lamb chops, cleaned, washed, pat-dried	16
For the first marinade:	
Raw papaya paste for tenderizing	4'' x 4''
Ginger-garlic (*adrak-lasan*) paste	1 tbsp / 18 gm
Red chilli paste	1 tbsp / 15 gm
Ginger juice	1¹/₂ tbsp
Salt to taste	
Vinegar (*sirka*)	2 tsp / 10 ml
Vegetable oil	2 tsp / 10 ml
For the second marinade:	
Yoghurt (*dahi*), hung, whisked	1 cup / 250 gm / 9 oz
Ginger-garlic paste	1 tbsp / 18 gm
Ginger juice	4 tbsp
Ginger, chopped	2 tbsp / 15 gm
Salt to taste	
Garam masala	1 tbsp / 9 gm
Yellow chilli powder	3 tsp / 9 gm
Vegetable oil	5 tsp / 25 ml

Melted butter for basting

Method:

1. **For the first marinade**, mix all the ingredients together and apply over the lamb chops. Rub well and marinate for 2-3 hours.
2. **For the second marinade**, mix the ingredients in the order listed. Squeeze the extra moisture from the marinated chops and put them in the above marinade. Keep aside for 3-4 hours.
3. Skewer the lamb chops 1'' apart by piercing from the meat and along the bone so that it does not fall. Roast in a tandoor or over a charcoal grill at a moderate temperature for 12-15 minutes. Hang the skewer to let the extra moisture drain off completely. Baste with melted butter and further roast for 4-6 minutes.
4. Serve hot with choice of salad and chutney.

Marinated cubes roasted on skewers

Bihari kebabs

Preparation time: 6 hrs. Cooking time: 10-15 min. Serves: 4

Ingredients:

Undercut for beef, cut into 1″ x 3″ strips	500 gm / 1.1 lb
For the marinade:	
Onions, ground to a paste	2
Garlic (*lasan*) cloves	5
Ginger (*adrak*)	2″ piece
Raw papaya	2″ piece
Cinnamon (*dalchini*)	2″ piece
Green cardamom (*choti elaichi*)	2
Black cardamom (*moti elaichi*)	2
Black peppercorns (*sabut kali mirch*)	6
Allspice berries	6
Vegetable oil	2 tbsp / 30 ml / 1 fl oz
Salt to taste	

Method:

1. **For the marinade**: mix all the ingredients together and rub well into the meat. Keep aside for 6 hours.
2. Thread the pieces of meat though a skewer and pack them together. One long skewer should hold 5 strips of meat. Turn over glowing coals for 10-15 minutes, basting once or twice with oil.
3. Do not over cook, as the meat is very tender and will fall off the skewer.
4. Slide the kebabs off the skewer on to a plate and serve with lemon wedges, onion rings, and green chillies.

Roast leg of lamb flavoured with yoghurt

Raan

Preparation time: 2¹/₂ hrs. Cooking time: 2 hrs. Serves: 4

Ingredients:

Lamb, leg piece	1
For the marinade:	
Brown onion paste	4 tbsp / 100 gm / 3¹/₂ oz
Garlic (*lasan*) paste	2 tsp / 12 gm
Ginger (*adrak*) paste	2 tsp / 12 gm
Green cardamom (*choti elaichi*) powder	¹/₂ tsp / 1¹/₂ gm
Yoghurt (*dahi*)	4 tbsp / 120 gm / 6 gm
Red chilli powder	2 tsp / 6 gm
Salt to taste	
Garam masala	¹/₂ tsp / 1¹/₂ gm
Black pepper (*kali mirch*) powder	1 tsp / 3 gm
Saffron (*kesar*)	a pinch
Vegetable oil for basting	
Chaat masala to taste	

Method:

1. Clean the leg of lamb and prick thoroughly down to the bone with a fork. Mix all the ingredients of the marinade together. Apply evenly on the lamb and leave to marinate for 2 hours.

2. Place leg in a baking tray with 2 cups water. Bake in a preheated (180°C / 350°F) oven for at least 1 hour turning the leg twice / thrice to ensure that the leg cooks evenly. Roast till the liquid dries up.

3. Baste with oil and grill / roast in a moderately hot tandoor till well done.

4. Sprinkle *chaat* masala and garnish with onion rings. Serve with mint and coriander chutney (see p. 95).

lamb

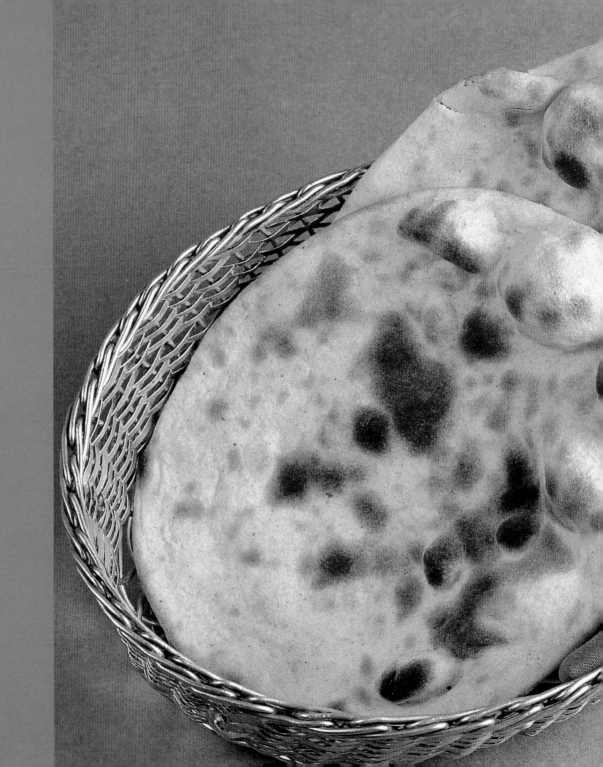

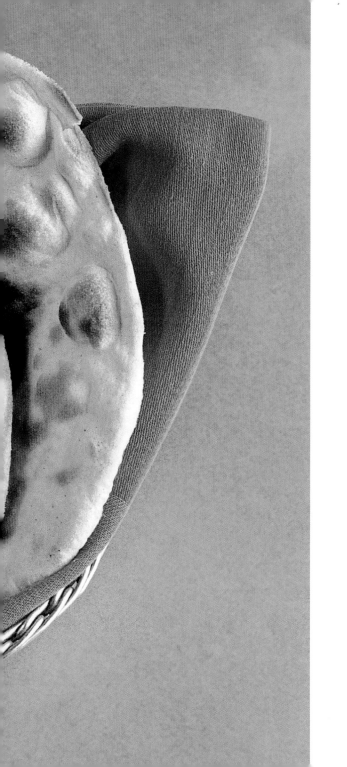

accompaniments

Unleavened, wholewheat bread

Tandoori roti

Preparation time: 30 min. Cooking time: 30 min. Serves: 4

Ingredients:

Wholewheat flour (*atta*)   2 cups / 300 gm / 11 oz
Ghee for greasing baking tray
Refined flour (*maida*) for dusting
Salt to taste

Method:

1. Sieve the wholewheat flour with salt onto a kneading platter.
2. Make a well in the flour and pour approximately 1$^1/_2$ cups water into it. Knead to a soft dough.
3. Cover with a damp cloth and keep aside for 20 minutes.
4. Divide the dough equally into 8 balls and dust with flour.
5. Pat and flatten each ball with the palms to make 6"-wide discs.
6. Using oven gloves, stick the disc to the side of a moderately hot tandoor. Bake for 2 minutes then peel off swiftly. Alternatively, place on a greased baking tray and bake for 5-6 minutes at 180°C / 350°F in a preheated oven.
7. Serve hot with any curry.

Leavened bread

Khameeri roti

Preparation time: 1 hr. Cooking time: 20 min. Serves: 4

Ingredients:

Wholewheat flour (*atta*)	2 cups / 300 gm / 11 oz
Salt to taste	
Yeast, fresh, dissolved in $^1/_2$ cup warm water	$1^1/_2$ tsp
Ghee for greasing baking tray	
Refined flour (*maida*) for dusting	

Method:

1. Sieve the wholewheat flour with salt. Pour 1 cup water and knead into a tough dough. Cover with a damp cloth and keep aside for 15 minutes.
2. Slowly sprinkle the dissolved yeast over the dough and keep kneading till the dough is smooth and pliable and not sticky. Cover with a damp cloth and keep aside for 30 minutes.
3. Divide the dough into 8 equal balls and dust with dry flour.
4. Press and flatten each ball into round discs, 8" wide. Using oven gloves, stick the disc to the side of a hot tandoor and bake for 2 minutes. Remove with a pair of tongs. Alternatively, place on a greased baking tray and bake for 4-5 minutes in a preheated oven at 180°C / 350°F. Serve hot.

accompaniments

Leavened bread with onion seeds

Naan

Preparation time: 2½ hrs. Cooking time: 15 min. Serves: 4

Ingredients:

Refined flour (*maida*)	2 cups / 280 gm / 10 oz
Salt to taste	
Baking soda	¼ tsp
Baking powder	1 tsp / 6 gm
Whisk together:	
Milk	3 tbsp / 45 ml / 1½ fl oz
Sugar	2 tsp / 6 gm
Yoghurt (*dahi*)	5 tsp / 25 gm
Groundnut oil	2 tbsp / 30 ml / 1 fl oz
Onion seeds (*kalonji*)	1 tsp / 3 gm
Melon (*magaz*) seeds	1 tsp / 2 gm
Ghee for greasing tray	
White butter	2 tbsp / 30 gm / 1 oz

Method:

1. Sieve first 4 ingredients onto a kneading platter. Make a well in the centre; mix in 1 cup water and milk mixture and knead to make a dough. Cover with a moist cloth and keep aside for 10 minutes.

2. Add oil and knead again. Cover the dough and keep aside for 2 hours till it rises. Divide the dough into 6 balls. Flatten balls and sprinkle onion and melon seeds. Cover and keep aside for 5 minutes.

3. Roll and flatten each ball between your palms. Stretch dough to one side to give an elongated shape. Using oven gloves, stick the *naan* inside a hot tandoor for 3 minutes or place the *naan* on a greased tray and bake in an oven for 10 minutes at 180°C / 350°F. Apply butter (optional) and serve.

accompaniments

94

Mint and coriander chutney

Pudina-dhaniya chutney

Preparation time: 20 min.

Ingredients:

Green coriander (*hara dhaniya*)	1 cup / 60 gm / 2 oz
Mint (*pudina*) leaves	1 cup / 35 gm / 1 oz
Curry leaves *(kadhi patta)*	¹/₂ cup
Green chillies	6-8
Cumin *(jeera)* seeds	2 tsp / 4 gm
Sugar	¹/₂ cup / 100 gm / 3¹/₂ oz
Tamarind (*imli*) extract	¹/₂ cup
Salt	2 tsp / 6 gm

Method:

1. Blend all the ingredients together with 2-3 tbsp water into a smooth paste.
2. Use as required.

index

ACCOMPANIMENTS

Leavened bread   93
Leavened bread with onion seeds   94
Mint and coriander chutney   95
Unleavened, wholewheat bread   92

CHICKEN

Barbecued chicken   55
Cardamom flavoured chicken drumsticks   56
Cheesy chicken kebabs   46
Chicken breasts stuffed
   with minced lamb   60
Chicken drumsticks with beetroot   51
Chicken drumsticks coated
   with cashew batter   52
Chicken kebabs flavoured with fenugreek   65
Chicken tikka marinated in cottage cheese   48
Creamy chicken tikkas   50
Delicate chicken kebabs
   with a hint of fenugreek   44
Skewered chicken   59
Stuffed tandoori drumsticks   62

FISH & OTHER SEAFOOD

Barbecued prawns in a rich
   and creamy marinade   32
Fish tikkas   28
Roasted prawns coated
   with sesame seeds   40
Smoked fish chunks   30
Saffron flavoured fish rolls stuffed
   with prawns   34

Tandoori fish in yoghurt marinade   37
Tandoori lobsters   41
Tandoori prawns   38

LAMB

Barbecued lamb liver and kidney
   covered with chicken mince   74
Cinnamon flavoured ribs   72
Ginger flavoured lamb chops   86
Lamb kebabs stuffed with cheese   70
Marinated cubes roasted on skewers   87
Melt-in-the-mouth skewered kebabs   83
Roast leg of lamb flavoured with yoghurt   88
Skewered lamb chops   80
Spicy and aromatic lamb chunks   68
Spicy lamb steaks   73
Spicy minced meat skewered and roasted   78
Succulent lamb chunks coated
   with papaya and yoghurt   76
Tangy mint lamb chops   84
Thin meat slices roasted on skewers   82

VEGETARIAN

Barbecued potato rolls   14
Cottage cheese cubes flavoured
   with fenugreek   18
Cottage cheese slices layered with
   mint and coriander chutney   20
Roasted batter fried cauliflower   24
Skewered cottage cheese kebabs   16
Stuffed capsicum   17
Stuffed potato rectangles   22